You're Either One or The Other

A Children's Book about Human Sexuality

by

Joy Wilt

Illustrated by Ernie Hergenroeder

Educational Products Division
Word, Incorporated
Waco, Texas

Author

JOY WILT is creator and director of Children's Ministries, an organization that provides resources "for people who care about children"—speakers, workshops, demonstrations, consulting services, and training institutes. A certified elementary school teacher, administrator, and early childhood specialist, Joy is also consultant to and professor in the master's degree program in children's ministries for Fuller Theological Seminary. Joy is a graduate of LaVerne College, LaVerne, California (B.A. in Biological Science), and Pacific Oaks College, Pasadena, California (M.A. in Human Development). She is author of three books, *Happily Ever After, An Uncomplicated Guide to Becoming a Superparent,* and *Taming the Big Bad Wolves,* as well as the popular *Can-Make-And-Do Books.* Joy's commitment "never to forget what it feels like to be a child" permeates the many innovative programs she has developed and her work as lecturer, consultant, writer, and—not least—mother of two children, Christopher and Lisa.

Artist

ERNIE HERGENROEDER is founder and owner of Hergie & Associates (a visual communications studio and advertising agency). With the establishment of this company in 1975, "Hergie" and his wife, Faith, settled in San Jose with their four children, Lynn, Kathy, Stephen, and Beth. Active in community and church affairs, Hergie is involved in presenting creative workshops for teachers, ministers, and others who wish to understand the techniques of communicating visually. He also lectures in high schools to encourage young artists toward a career in commercial art. Hergie serves as a consultant to organizations such as the Police Athletic League (PAL), Girl Scouts, and religious and secular corporations. His ultimate goal is to touch the hearts of kids (8 to 80) all over the world—visually!

ISBN: 0-8499-8143-3
Library of Congress Catalog Card Number: 79-52203
Bruce Johnson, Editor

The educational concepts presented in the Ready-Set-Grow book series are also featured in a music songbook and longplay record. For further information concerning these materials see your local bookstore or write Word, Incorporated, 4800 West Waco Drive, Waco, Texas 76710.

Contents

Introduction

You're Either One or the Other is one of a series of books. The complete set is called *Ready-Set-Grow!*

You're Either One or the Other deals with human sexuality and can be used by itself or as a part of a program that utilizes all of the *Ready-Set-Grow!* books.

You're Either One or the Other is specifically designed so that children can either read the book or have it read to them. This can be done at home, church or school. When reading to children, it is not necessary to complete the book at one sitting. Concern should be given to the attention span of the individual child and his or her comprehension of the subject matter.

You're Either One or the Other is designed to involve the child in the concepts that are being taught. This is done by simply and carefully explaining each concept and then asking questions that invite a response from the child. It is hoped that by answering the questions, the child will personalize the concept and, thus, integrate it into his or her thinking.

You're Either One or the Other teaches that everyone is either male or female with obvious physical differences. There is no question that we are born with our physical differences. Emotional and personality traits, however, are thought to be either biologically or culturally based, or both, depending on whose doing the thinking.

At any rate it is not the purpose of this book to try to solve this continuing debate. Whatever the reasons for these differences, today's children are still pressured by society and peers into hiding certain personality traits considered improper for their sex. Boys face ridicule, for example, if they admit to feelings of tenderness. An aggressive girl is often called a "tomboy" (whatever that means).

You're Either One or the Other is designed to help children understand that a mature personality possesses a balance of what are considered masculine and feminine qualities without losing one's identity as either male or female. This is what it means to be a "whole" person. Children who grow up learning this will be better equipped to live healthy, productive lives.

You're Either One or the Other

You're either one or the other.

Do you know what it means to be one or the other?

If you do not know what it means to be
one or the other, that's OK because . . .

this book will tell you all about it.

To begin with . . .

Chapter 1

You Are a Person

You are a person, and because that's true . . .

you're either male or female.

A male person can be either a boy or a man.

A female person can be either a girl or a woman.

A boy is a male child.

A boy grows up . . .

and becomes a man.

A man is a male adult.

A girl is a female child.

A girl grows up . . .

and becomes a woman.

A woman is a female adult.

So, you are either one or the other, male or female.

Which are you?   Male_____   Female___✓_____

How do you know?

First of all . . .

Chapter 2

What Is a Boy?

Remember, a boy is a male child.

Every male has a penis.

The penis looks like a short tube between the legs.

Every male also has a scrotum and testicles.

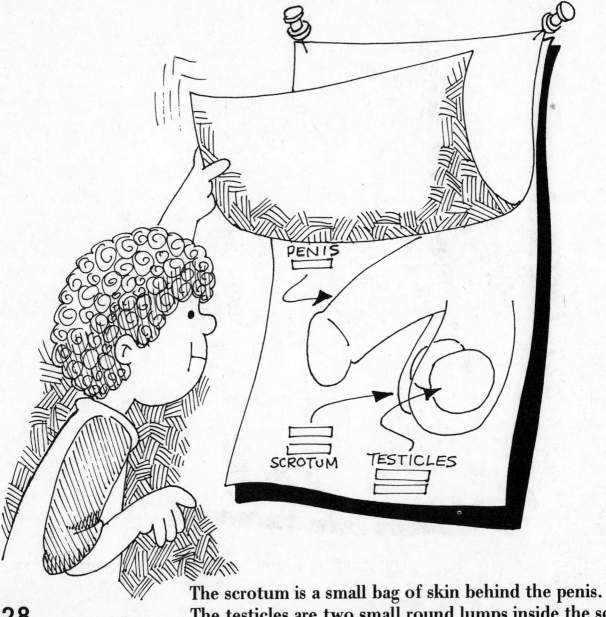

The scrotum is a small bag of skin behind the penis.
The testicles are two small round lumps inside the scrotum

So one of the things being a boy means is having a penis and testicles.

Being a boy means other things, too.

Boys often look, act, and think differently from girls.

But some people say all boys should always look, act, and think in certain ways. This isn't true.

Each boy is a special person. No one else in the world is exactly like him.

There are many different ways for boys to be that are OK.

For example . . .

33

There are hundreds of names that boys can have.

Most boys have names that are different from girls' names.

But some boys have names that can be girls' names, too.

Boys can like any color they choose to like.

Terry's favorite color is blue.
He wears blue clothes
almost all the time.

36

But Tom doesn't like blue. He prefers to wear red and pink. **37**

A boy can decide for himself whether or not he wants to wear jewelry.

Kim doesn't like jewelry, so he doesn't wear any.

But Jeff wears a necklace.

Boys can use their bodies in different ways.

Danny uses his muscles to lift weights.

But Gary is learning to be graceful.

Some boys like to play sports, while other boys do not.

Jonny, Howie, and Ken like playing sports better than anything else.

But Aaron and Bob don't like sports. They would rather spend their free time in other ways.

Some boys like to play outdoors. Other boys prefer to stay inside.

Terry likes winter sports. Snow skiing is one of his favorite outdoor activities.

But Joe would much rather stay inside by a warm fire and read a good book.

There are hundreds of things that boys can be when they grow up.

Sam wants to be an airplane mechanic. Stacy wants to be a policeman. Chuck wants to be a businessman.

Kirk wants to be a teacher. Lionel wants to be a nurse.
Chip wants to be a librarian.

So . . .

There are many different ways for boys to be that are OK.

Boys can have names that are only boys' names, or they can have names that are sometimes girls' names.

Boys can like any color they choose to like.

Boys can decide for themselves whether or not they want to wear jewelry.

Boys can use their bodies in many different ways.

Boys can like sports, or they can like doing other things better.

Boys can like to be outdoors, or they can prefer to stay inside.

Boys can decide for themselves what they want to be when they grow up.

Can you think of other ways that are OK for a boy to be?

What are you? Are you a boy?

How can you tell whether or not you are a boy?

If you are a boy, being a boy is part of who you are. But remember that no other boy is exactly like you. So what being a boy means to you is different from what it means to anyone else.

What does it mean to you to be a boy?

How does it feel?

What do you like best about being a boy?

What do you like least?

As you grow and learn, you will find out a great deal more about what it means to you to be a boy. Many of the things you learn will be things that no one else can teach you. You will learn them from what you do, what happens to you, and how you feel.

And some day, you will become a man.

Chapter 3

What Is a Man?

Remember, every boy grows up and becomes a man. Just
as there are many ways boys can be that are OK . . .

there are many ways men can be that are OK.

For example . . .

Men can get married and become fathers, they can get married and not have children, or they can stay single.

Mr. Thomas is married to Mrs. Thomas. He's the father of five children.

But Mr. Anderson is not married and not a father.

Men can do all sorts of things to help take care of their homes and families.

Mr. Young works in the yard and fixes up the house.

Mr. Franker cooks, cleans house, and takes care of his children.

Some men know how to fix things, but others don't.

Mr. Gray can fix a leaky pipe and lots of other things that go wrong around the house.

But Mr. Owen has to call someone for help when something goes wrong at his house.

Some men don't sew, while others sew very well.

Mr. Wallace never learned to sew. His wife does all his sewing for him.

But Mr. Smith likes to make his own shirts, and he does a very good job.

Some men don't like to go shopping, but others do.

Mr. Barnard's wife buys all his clothes for him, because he doesn't like to shop.

But Mr. Walker loves to shop and buys all his own clothes.

Some men take charge in difficult situations; other men do not.

Mr. Robinson is always glad to step in whenever someone in his family has a problem to handle.

But Mr. McCall is glad when the other people in his family handle problems themselves.

So . . .

There are many different ways for men to be that are OK.

Men can get married and become fathers, they can get married and not have children, or they can stay single.

Men can do all sorts of things to help take care of their homes and families.

Men can know how to fix things, or they can ask for help.

Men can learn how to sew, or they can ask someone else to do their sewing for them.

Men can do their own shopping, or they can let someone else do it.

Men can take charge in difficult situations, or they can allow other people to take charge.

Can you think of other ways that are OK for a man to be?

What will you grow up to be?

Will you grow up to be a man?

How do you know whether or not you will be a man when you grow up?

Remember, you are either one or the other, male or female; boy or girl.

If you are a boy, you are a male person and will someday grow up to be a man.

But what if you are a girl?

70

Chapter 3

What Is a Girl?

Remember, a girl is a female child.

Every female has labia and a vagina.

The labia are the two folds of skin between the legs.

The vagina is the small opening between the folds of skin.

74

So one of the things being a girl means is having labia, a vagina, and other important organs inside the body.

Being a girl means other things, too.

Girls often look, act, and think differently from boys.

But some people say all girls should always look, act, and think in certain ways. This isn't true.

Each girl is a special person. No one else in the world is exactly like her.

There are many different ways for girls to be that are OK.

For example . . .

There are hundreds of names that girls can have.

Most girls have names that are different from boys' names.

But some girls have names that can be boys' names, too.

Girls can like any color they choose to like.

Melinda wears pink clothes very often because pink is her
favorite color.

But Mandy likes to wear blue.

Girls can wear different kinds of clothes.

Cheryl always wears dresses.

But Wendy often wears pants.

Girls can use their bodies in different ways.

Mikie is learning to be a ballet dancer.

Carol likes to run and climb trees.

Some girls like to play sports, while other girls do not.

Nanette is a great basketball player.

But Helen isn't interested in sports. She would rather spend her free time in other ways.

Some girls like to stay inside, while others prefer to be outdoors.

Ellen's favorite place to play is her own room.

But Shawn loves to play outdoors and explore new places where she's never been before.

There are hundreds of things that girls can be when they grow up.

Marilyn wants to be a housewife. Debbie wants to be a secretary.
Sharon wants to be a telephone operator.

Candace wants to be a doctor. Leah wants to be a firefighter.
Jody wants to be an airplane pilot.

So . . .

There are many different ways for girls to be that are OK.

Girls can have names that are only girls' names, or they can have names that are sometimes boys' names.

Girls can like any color they choose to like.

Girls can wear dresses and skirts all the time, or they can wear pants.

Girls can use their bodies in many different ways.

Girls can like sports, or they can like doing other things better.

Girls can like to stay inside, or they can prefer to be outdoors.

Girls can decide for themselves what they want to be when they grow up.

Can you think of other ways that are OK for a girl to be?

What are you?   Are you a girl?

How can you tell whether or not you are a girl?

If you are a girl, being a girl is part of who you are. But remember that no other girl is exactly like you. So what being a girl means to you is different from what it means to anyone else.

What does it mean to you to be a girl?

How does it feel?

What do you like best about being a girl?

What do you like least?

As you grow and learn, you will find out a great deal more about what it means to you to be a girl. Many of the things you learn will be things that no one else can teach you. You will learn them from what you do, what happens to you, and how you feel.

And some day, you will be a woman.

Chapter 5

What Is a Woman?

Remember, every girl grows up and becomes a woman. Just as there are many ways girls can be that are OK . . .

there are many ways women can be that are OK.

For example . . .

Women can get married and become mothers, they can get married and not have children, or they can stay single.

Ms. Goldsmith is married to Mr. Goldsmith. She's the mother of three children.

Ms. Taylor is not married and not a mother.

Women can choose to work at home or away from home.

Ms. Ellis cleans house and watches her children while her husband works away from home earning money for the family.

But Ms. Daniels and her husband both take care of the house and children, and both of them work away from home to earn money for the family.

105

Women can do all sorts of things to help take care of their homes and families.

Ms. Jones cooks, cleans the house, and takes care of her children.

Ms. Peterson likes to work in the yard and fix up the house.

Some women don't know how to fix things when they break, but others do.

Ms. Meredith has to call someone for help when something goes wrong at her house.

Ms. Thompson can fix almost anything.

Some women do not have strong muscles, while others do.

Ms. Crashaw doesn't lift anything heavy, because she is sure she would hurt herself if she did.

Ms. Florence is very strong.

Women can enjoy the outdoors, or they can prefer not to "rough it."

A picnic in her backyard is about as rough as Ms. Williams ever wants to get.

Ms. Johnson loves to go camping in the mountains.

So . . .

There are many different ways for women to be that are OK.

Women can get married and become mothers, they can get married and not have children, or they can stay single.

Women can choose to work at home or away from home.

Women can do all sorts of things to help take care of their homes and families.

Women can know how to fix things when they break, or they can ask for help.

Some women do not have strong muscles, while others do.

Women can enjoy the outdoors, or they can prefer not to "rough it."

Can you think of other ways that are OK for a woman to be?

What will you grow up to be?

Will you grow up to be a woman?

How do you know whether or not you will be a woman when you grow up?

Remember, you are either one or the other, male or female; boy or girl.

If you are a girl, you are a female person and will someday grow up to be a woman.

Conclusion

So, what does it mean to be one or the other?

First, it means that you are either male or female; boy or girl.

If you are a boy, your body is different from a girl's body.

If you are a girl, your body is different from a boy's body.

122

Remember, whether you're a boy or a girl, nobody else is exactly like you. And nobody else can tell you exactly how you should look, act, or feel.

There are many ways boys and girls can be that are OK.

And because you are a special person, being a boy or girl is different for you than it is for anyone else.

As you grow and learn, you will find out more about what it means to you to be a boy or a girl.

You will learn some of these things from other people . . .

but some of them you can learn only from yourself.

And someday, you will become either a man or a woman.